AMAZING SPACE

Fun Facts for Curious Kids!

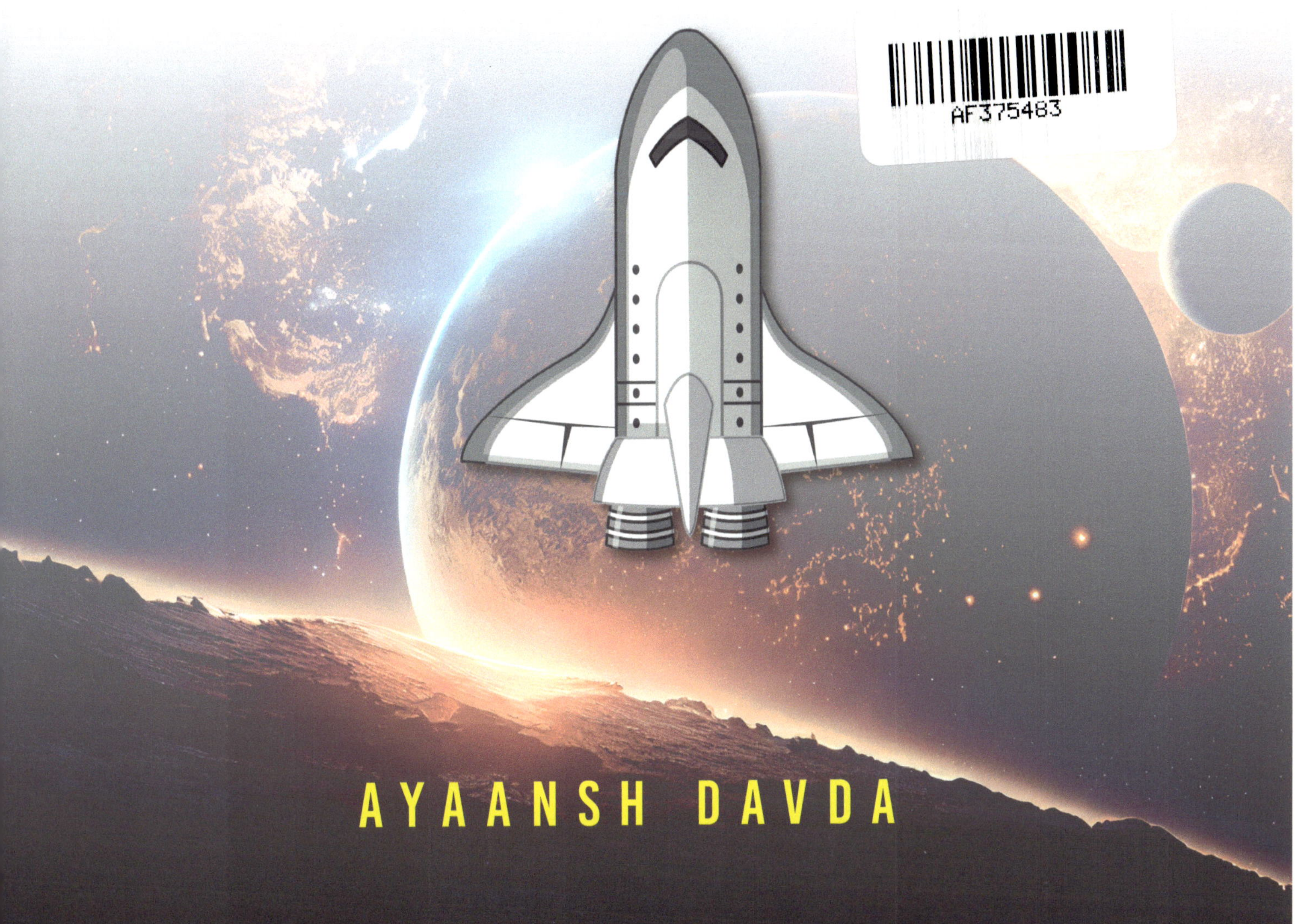

A Y A A N S H   D A V D A

USA
USA

FOREWORD

Welcome to the vast, mysterious world of space! In this book, you'll discover fun facts about our Solar System, stars, galaxies, and more! Prepare for a journey that's out of this world!

Dedicated to

Dadi

PLANETS

PLANETS: FRIENDS OF THE SUN

 Mercury is the smallest planet and closest to the Sun.

 Venus has crushing air pressure, much stronger than Earths.

 Earth is the only known planet with life!

 Mars is known as the red planet because of its iron-rich soil.

 Jupiter's Storms are as big as 2 Earths.

 Saturn's stunning rings are made of ice and rock.

 Uranus spins on its side and is the second coldest planet.

 Neptune has powerful storms like Jupiter.

Sun
Earth
Jupiter
Saturn
Venus
Neptune
Uranus
Mercury
Mars

TABLE OF CONTENTS

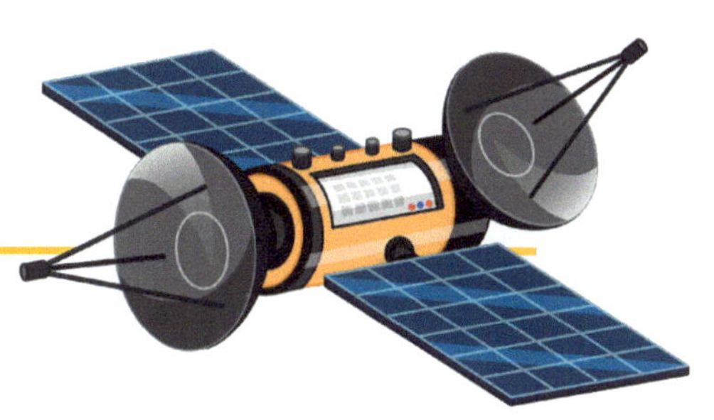

Our Solar System

Neptune

Uranus

Saturn

Jupiter

Our Universe started with an explosion called the Big Bang. Before the explosion, it was called the Cosmic Egg!

Did you know our Solar System has eight planets, not nine?

There are eight planets in our Solar System not nine. (Pluto is not considered as a planet but it was considered as a planet until 2007) and one star, the Sun which gives us heat and light every day. It is the nearest star to Earth at the distance of 93 million miles.

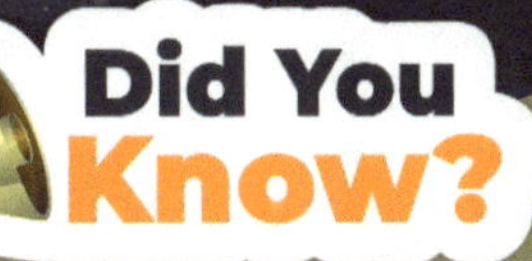

Our Solar System is made up of eight planets and one star – the Sun! These planets revolve around the Sun, which is why we have days, nights, and seasons.

Did you know our Universe (the place where our Earth, Solar System, Meteors etc are there) is 13.8 billion years old!

I still don't know how they figured it out!

Mars

Earth

Venus

Mercury

There are more than 200 Moons in the Solar System.

There are more than 200 Moons in the Solar System. Saturn has 148 Moons and Jupiter has 94 Moons. Neptune has 16. Uranus has 28, Mars has 2 and Earth has 1. All the Moons orbit planets. Venus and Mercury have no Moons as their gravity is very less but Pluto has 5 Moons, (even though it is not a planet) and many more unconfirmed Moons.

More than a 100 trillion Suns can fit in the biggest star in the Milky Way.

Which means.

1 Sun = 1,000 Jupiters

1 Jupiter = 1,300 Earths

13,00,000 trillion Earths can fit in the biggest star in the Milky way

Did You Know?

There are two asteroid belts in our Solar System. Asteroid belt are belts of asteroids which are making a kind of barrier to the inner and outer planets of the Solar System, that is the asteroid belt between Mars and Jupiter. The asteroid belt beside Neptune, separates the Solar System from other stars and planets.

Our Solar System expands by 75.5 kilometers per second!

This is super fast. After the big bang, the universe has been expanding a lot.

Our Universe expands by 75 kilometers per second!

This means that 4,500 kms per minute. This universe is expanding too fast!!

There are more than 1,000 confirmed exoplanets and 1 trillion more to be discovered!

Exoplanets are planets that orbit stars outside our Solar System. Till now its estimated that 1 trillion exoplanets are to be confirmed. 1000 exoplanets are confirmed.

The largest Moon is Ganymede of Jupiter in our Solar System.

It is even bigger than Mercury, it is 3,125 miles long. It might have oceans on its surface too!

There could be many other universes called the Multiverse.

Experts think that they might have bigger celestial objects.

All the planets' names are Mercury, Venus, Earth, Mars, Jupiter, Saturn, Uranus, and Neptune.

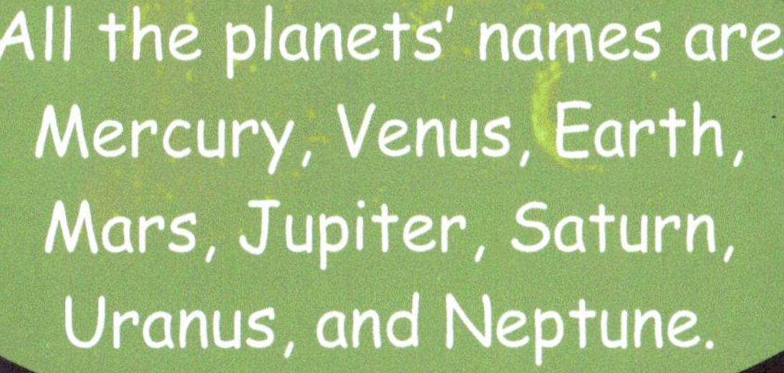

They have their own qualities.

Sirius B has exploded/died in a supernova!

Sirius B, the twin of Sirius A is now a white dwarf. It will then become a black dwarf. The centre of the star can survive as a neutral star or a black hole.

There are almost 3,083 comets in the Solar System.

It includes Hailey's comet, Hale-Bopp, which developed 6 tails. It also includes Shoemaker Levy-9, which collided into Jupiter and this was the biggest collision seen by mankind!

Dwarf planets are bodies which orbit a star but are too small to be considered as a planet.

Did you know Mercury and Venus do not have any Moons?

They have very less gravity to capture any Moon and make them revolve around them. Even if they had a Moon, the larger bodies of the Solar System with a larger gravitational force would attract them.

There are 5 dwarf planets: Ceres, Pluto, Haumea, Makemake, and Eris.

Some people live in space on the International Space Station (ISS) from all over the world.

Some people stay in space like a vacation. It is called the International Space Station. It is very rare to wash your hair in the ISS. They sleep in beds tied to the walls with seat belts, so you do not fly away. Their food is normal but sometimes dehydrated which means you have to put water in it.

It is now the first human made object to land on a celestial body. It stayed on the line for five hours. It stayed longer than anyone could imagine.

The space shuttle Huygens was the first one to land on one of Saturn's Moons, Titan.

Ceres is the largest asteroid located in the asteroid belt between Mars and Jupiter, while the others, like Pluto, Haumea, Makemake, and Eris, are farther out near Neptune in a region called the Kuiper Belt.

Ceres, Pluto, Haumea, Makemake, and Eris are in the asteroid belt.

Pluto-Moons

Pluto has 5 Moons: Charon, Nix, Styx, Kerberos, and Hydra.

Charon is the largest Moon of Pluto. Nix and Hydra were discovered in 2005.

Jupiter and Saturn have a lot of Moons.

They have strong gravity which helps them to get more Moons. They are always fighting that who becomes the King of Moons.

Our Milky Way belongs to a group called the Local Group.

Saturn is the king of Moons. It has 148!

They have different shaped Moons such as Titan, Hyperion, Janus, Pandora etc.

It is a group of more than 50 galaxies. Andromeda and Milky Way might even combine to make a giant galaxy!

The Solar System is 4.6 billion years old

It formed some billion years after the universe formed. The universe is 13.8 billion years old.

Europa, Jupiter's largest Moon, was discovered by Galileo Galilei.

He is credited of discovering it though Siman Marius claimed to discover it in 1601.

Saturn is the second biggest planet in our Solar System.

It is 72,367 miles long which makes it the second largest planet in the Solar System. Saturn is very light and can float in water.

Uranus is the coldest planet in the Solar System.

It has a temperature of -224 degrees Celsius! It is so cold because of its distance from the Sun.

An asteroid killed all the dinosaurs 65 million years ago in Mexico.

People think that an asteroid wiped out dinosaurs 65 million years ago. There is even a crater in Mexico which is used like proof.

Neil Armstrong was the first one to step on the Moon. He stepped first with his left foot, with Buzz Aldrin following him.

There was a race between Soviet Union and the USA to be the first country to reach the Moon.

Mars is named after the God of War because of its red color.

Because of this blood-like color, the ancient Romans named it after their god of war, Mars.

Jupiter is named after the King of the Gods.

Because of its large size, it is named after the Roman King of Gods. It can hold 1300 Earths.

Venus is named after the Goddess of Love.

This is because of its very shining appearance in the sky, which is the third brightest in the sky after the Sun and the Moon.

Neptune is named after the God of the Sea.

Because of its blue colour, it is named after the God of the Sea. It takes 165 Earth years to orbit the Sun since its discovery in 1846. It has completed an orbit in 2011.

Saturn is named after the Roman God of Agriculture and wealth.

Saturn is named after the Roman God of Agriculture and wealth because the Romans name the brightest planets after important Gods.

Mercury is the messenger of the Gods.

He is known for his speed. Mercurians was a Roman God.

Uranus is named after a Greek God.

Uranus is named after the Greek God of Heavens. Uranus is the seventh planet from the Sun. Most of it is water.

FIRST QUARTER

WAXING GIBBOUS

WAXING CRESCENT

MOON
PHASES

NEW MOON

FULL MOON

WANING GIBBOUS

LAST QUARTER

WANING CRESCENT

All the Moons in the Solar System do not have their own light.

The Moons reflect the light given from the Sun.

PHASES OF THE MOON -

New Moon – We cannot see the new Moon from Earth.

Waxing Cresent – The Moon has moved a little, so we can see a small part of it from Earth.

First Quarter – The Moon has completed its first quarter around Earth. We can see the half-Moon at this time.

Waxing Gibbous – The Moon moves again and again. We can see more than half of the Moon. It is waxing or growing. Gibbous means it looks swollen on one side.

Full Moon – We can now see the full Moon. (its face)

Waning Gibbous – The Moon is a little more than half. It's shrinking or waning.

Last Quarter – The Moon is at is last quarter of the orbit around Earth.

Waning Crecent – The Moon has completed an orbit of the Earth.

Laika was a brave dog from Russia who became the first living creature to orbit Earth. In 1957, she was sent into space aboard a spacecraft called Sputnik 2. But she did not survive.

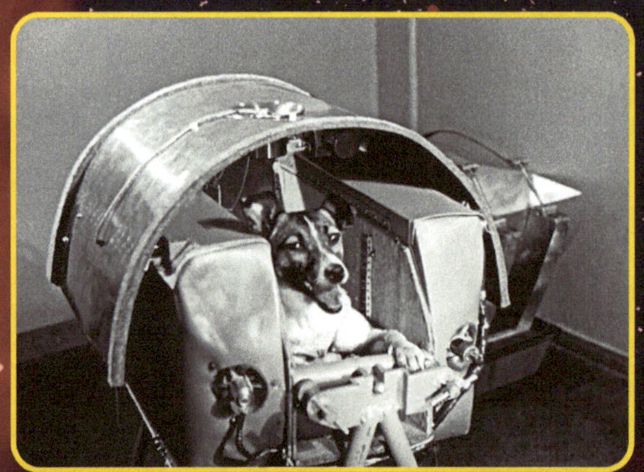

There are 70 trillion billion stars in space, and we can see 4,500 without a telescope or binoculars.

These stars are very bright, which are close, or far. There are so many stars, about 70 trillion billion stars. There might be more counting the ones in the multiverse also.

Our Milky Way is named by the Greeks. They called it a river of milk.

American stories tell of a dog dropping corn as he ran across the sky. Hindu Myth sees the Milky Way like the belly of a dolphin. Kalahari Bushmen say it was created by hot embers after a fire. Egyptians called the stars a pot of milk.

Some think there must be 100,000 million stars in the Milky Way galaxy. There might be even more.

A spacecraft would take billions of years to cross our galaxy. Our galaxy is very big.

When an asteroid came crashing into Earth in ancient times, people thought it was a punishment from the gods or fast dragons.

The ancient people thought all this but now we know what they are. Asteroids bring water and minerals to our planet.

Ceres is the largest asteroid in the Asteroid Belt.

Ceres is the size of France / Rajasthan or Texas (933km).

Comet means a long-haired star.

In Greek, comet means long-haired star as they thought the tail of the comet was hair.

A glove, rubbish bags, cameras, and nuts and bolts have been lost in space.

Because of this, Challenger, a spacecraft collided with this space junk and broke 73 seconds after launch.

Pluto is smaller than Eris and almost all the Moons, including our Moon.

Eris is 3,000 km (1,896 miles) long while our Moon is 3,100 km long. Even Pluto is smaller than our Moon.

Jupiter is 4.603 billion years old. It formed when the Solar System formed.

It saw how the Solar System evolved.

Saturn is 4.503 billion years old. Its rings are of the same age.

Uranus is the same age as Saturn. It is 4.503 billion years old.

It is also the same age as Neptune but it is younger than Mars, Earth and Jupiter.

Earth is 4.543 billion years old.

Earth is older than Saturn, Neptune and Uranus.

Neptune is the same age as Uranus and Saturn. It is 4.503 billion years old.

It is younger than Earth, Mars and Jupiter.

Mars is 4.603 billion years old, the same age as Jupiter

Mars is older than Earth, Saturn, Uranus, and Neptune.

Earth also had a ring, and all the meteors banged into each other, and the Moon was formed.

Earth also had a ring when it was forming. They believe a planet called Theia B collided with the Earth and the things which were remaining formed a ring around Earth. But they collided with each other and formed the Moon. (This is a theory)

Every star and planet rotates on its axis (an imaginary line).

For Earth this imaginary line is at 23.5 degrees. It helps the Earth with day and night and seasons. Sometimes stars orbit themselves like Sirus A and B. Planets orbit stars like Earth orbits the Sun.

Sirius A is the brightest star in the night sky.

Sirius A is the brightest star in the night sky even though it is 8 light years away from us.

When Earth was forming, a planet called Theia B collided with it, causing the axis to be tilted to 23.5 degrees.

This axis helps us in the day and night cycle and seasons. (This is a theory)

The rotation and revolution have caused day and night, seasonal cycles, and years, and even the Sun caused evaporation and ice formation and photosynthesis.

The biggest star in the Universe is in the Andromeda Galaxy.

It is so big that more than 10000 trillion Earths can fit inside it.

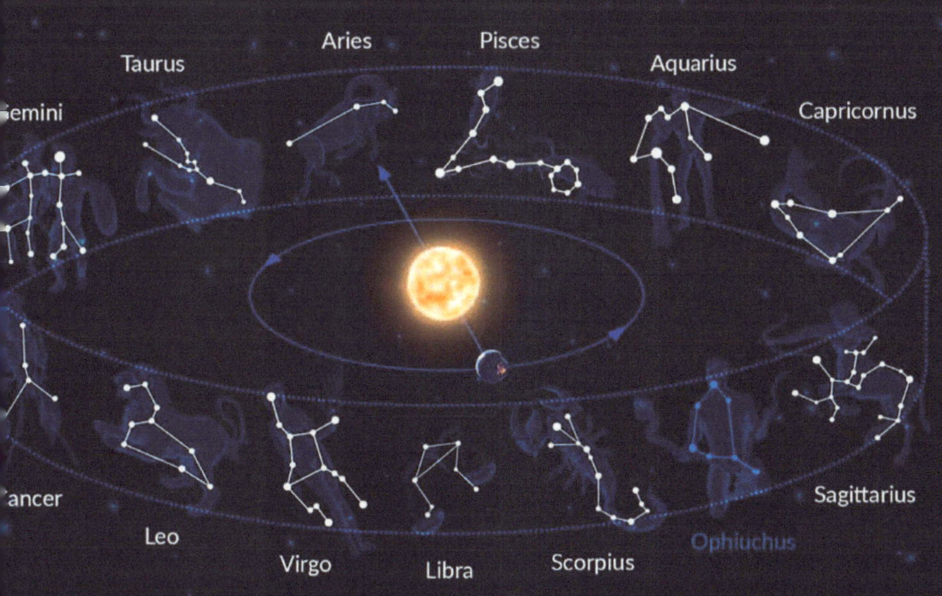

There are a lot of constellations like Leo the Lion, Orion the Hunter, Ursa Major the bear, Ursa Minor the dog, Cephus, which is half man and half horse and many more. Cephus is one of the largest constellations in the night sky.

Our fastest manned spacecraft, Helios, would take 19,000 years to reach the second nearest star, Proxima Centauri, which is 4.25 light-years (50 million kms) away.

Project Daedalus is planned and will reach Barnard's Star within 50 or fewer years.

It is 6 light years away.

Going between stars is called interstellar travel.

Travelling between galaxies is called intergalactic travel.

Daedalus will not be able to stop at Barnard's Star.

It will just take pictures and measurements about the star.

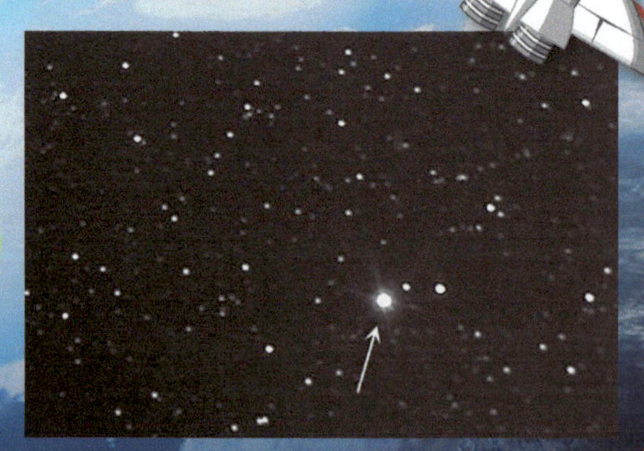

Woodpeckers delayed a space shuttle in 1995 by digging holes in the insulating foam. Plastic owls are used to scare them away.

The biggest and largest black holes are in the centre of the Andromeda Galaxy. It is called Ton 618. Black holes are holes that suck everything that comes in their path.

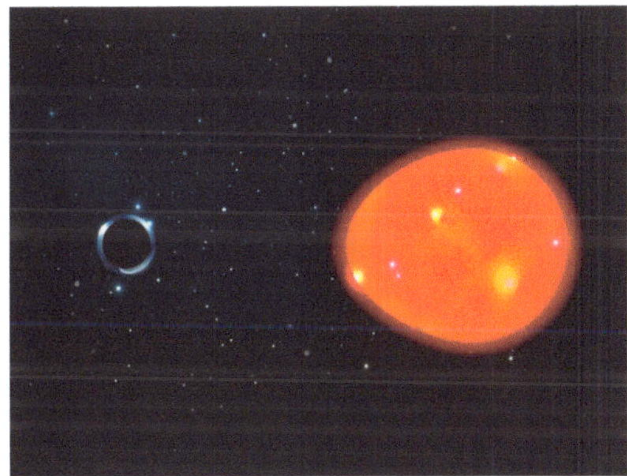

Unicorn is the black hole closest to Earth.

The black hole known as "The Unicorn" is the closest black hole to Earth. It's a small black hole compared to others and is located about 1,500 light-years away from us.

Black holes have special abilities: they fly freely in space, stay invisible, and suck things so fast that even light cannot pass through them, even though light is the fastest-moving object.

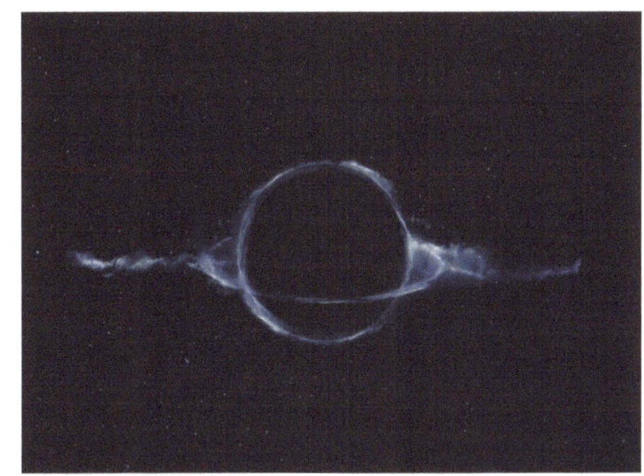

Light only take 8 minutes to reach Earth. The distance between the Sun and the Earth is 93 million miles.

Mercury takes only 88 days to orbit the Sun and is the nearest planet to the Sun.

If we are on Venus, a year is smaller than a week. It takes 223 Earth days to revolve around the Sun and it takes 243 Earth days to spin around its axis.

Time gets super slow when you are near a black hole. It acts like a sensor that a black hole is coming close.

The most epic UFO incident was in Roswell, which is a city in USA. They also saw a lot of debris, but they called it a flying disc in 1947.

The full form of UFO is Unidentified Flying Object, which means it is unidentified. The most UFO incidents are reports in USA. A farmer took a picture of a UFO which looked like a truck's mirror in Oregon 1950.

A Satellite has sent a message, and it will be delivered 25,000 years later to see if there are any aliens in M13. M13 is a cluster of stars.

You need to be away from artificial light/ polluted places to look at the space.

We can see the Betelgeuse star with the naked eye.

Betelgeuse is a giant red star that's nearing the end of its life, and one day it will explode in a supernova. It is in the Orion Constellation.

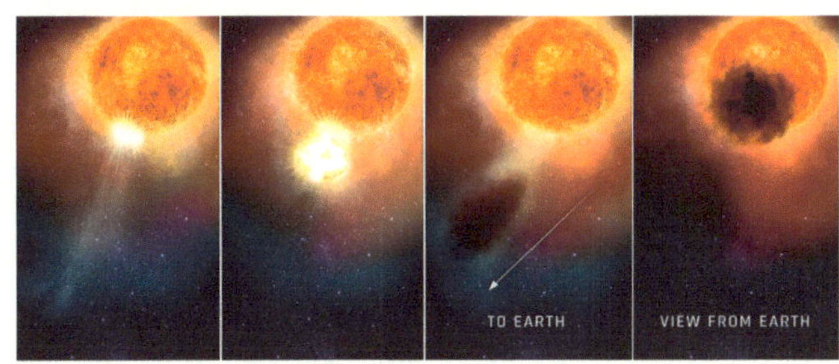

It is very rare to find constellations with our eyes.

But the basic ones like Orion and Leo are easy to see when there are no streetlamps and no pollution.

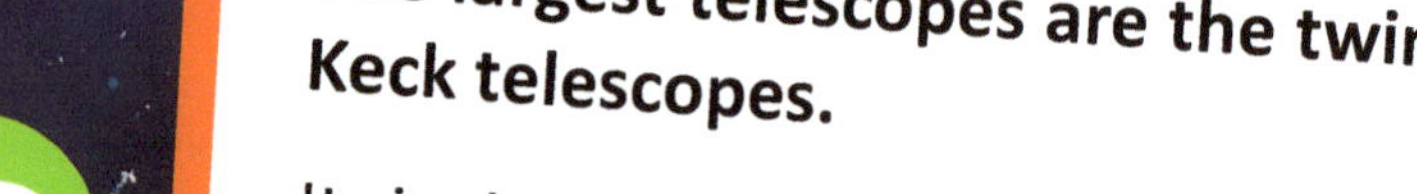

The largest telescopes are the twin Keck telescopes.

It is in Hawaii on Mount Kea a dormant and sleeping Volcano.

One light year is the distance light travels in a year.

In one year, it can travel almost 9.5 trillion kilometres (5.88 trillion miles)!

The James Webb telescope can look back in time, before the Big Bang, after the Big Bang, and study the Big Bang.

It was built in honour of James Webb, who was the 2nd administrator of NASA.

A storm on Earth is a breeze for Saturn.

Winds on Saturn can blow up to 1,800 kilometres per hour (1,100 miles per hour). We would be blown away by such winds.

The Sun is 100 times wider than the Earth and 10 times wider than Jupiter.

Saturn is wider than 3 Earths, 764 Earth's can fit within Saturn, 57 Earth's can fit inside Neptune, 1300 Earths can fit in Jupiter, 1.3 Million Earths can fit inside the Sun.

Mars till now has not shown signs of any life.

A lot of people think that there is life on Mars. Scientists have found a chemical which is only on planets which have life, and they found it on Venus and Mars, so they are thinking that humans must have changed planets.

Phobos

Deimos

Mars has two Moons, *Phobos* and *Deimos*.

Demos means terror in Greek and Phobos means fear in Greek.

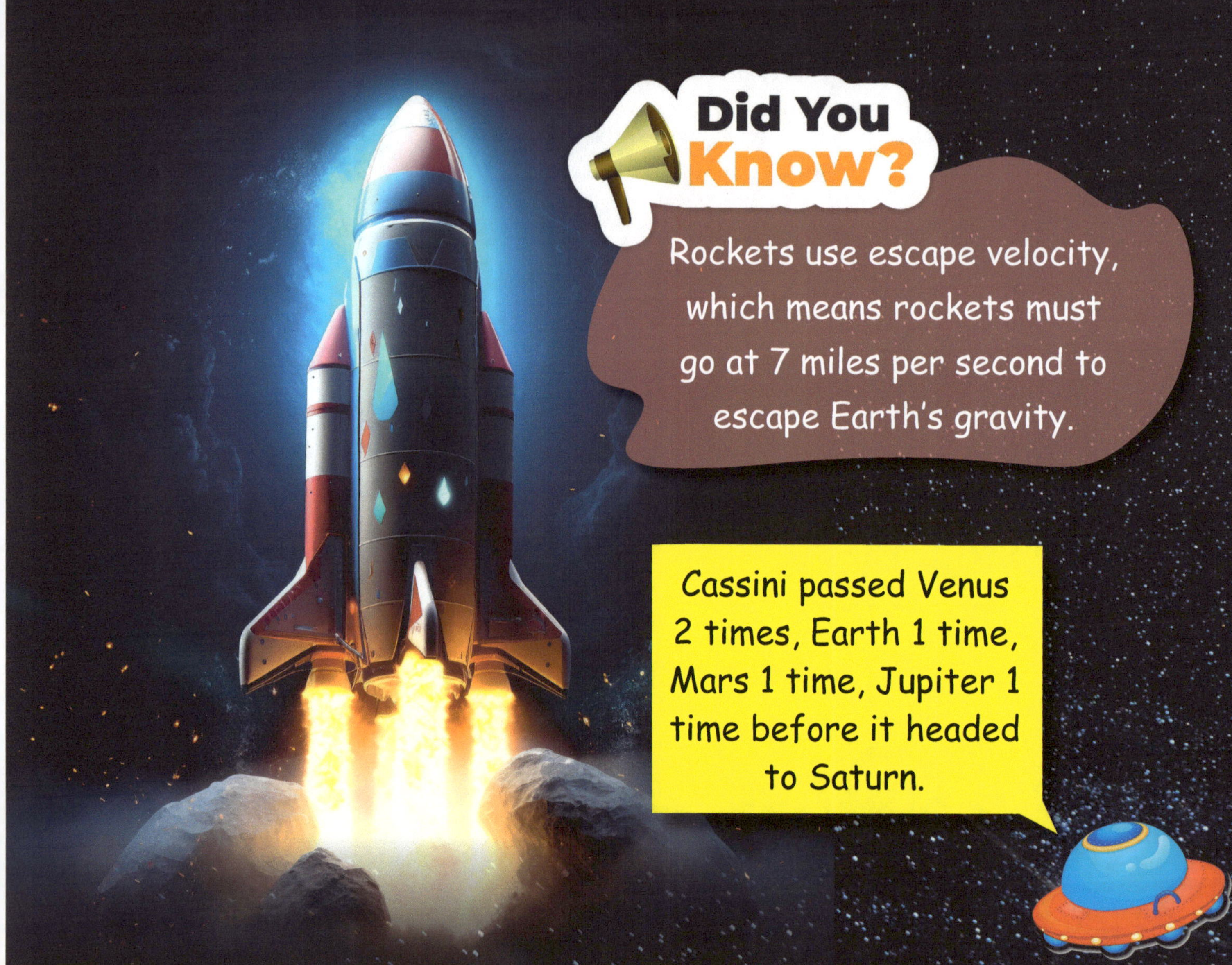

The Great Red Spot is actually a storm.

It could be the size of 2 Earths and is a very fast spinning storm.

Venus has crushing air pressure at its surface, more than 90 times that of Earth.

It is like being in a Pressurised cooker.

There are three storms on Neptune like Jupiter.

The three storms are Scooter, Great Dark Spot and Great Dark Spot 2.

Apollo 11 had only 71 KB of memory, and now calculators can store more than 500 KB.

The largest volcano is Olympus Mons on Mars.

Olympus Mons is the largest volcano not only on Mars but in the entire Solar System!

There is no sound in space because there is no air.

The Headphones are earbuds with radio equipment in helmets used to communicate in space.

Hubble is the size of a school bus.

It is exceedingly small.

Saturn's rings have seven layers.

The seven layers of rings are named A, B, C, D, E, F, and G, and they are separated by gaps called divisions. It is named in the order of when it was found.

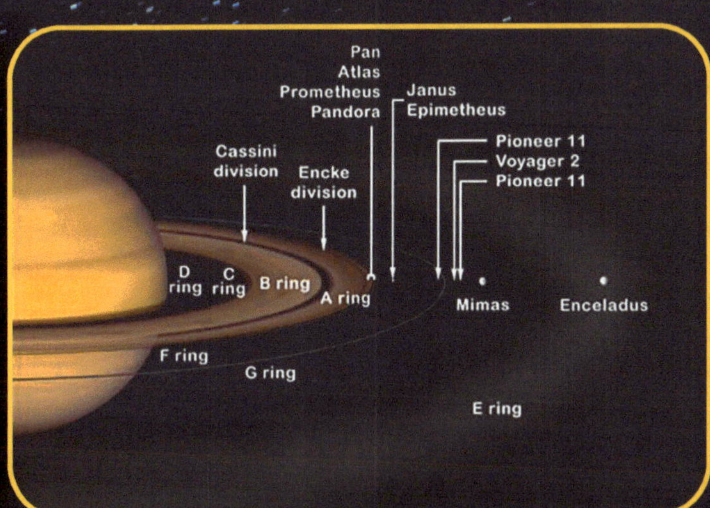

Uranus lacks a true surface and hosts extreme pressure and temperature that can destroy a metal rocket or spacecraft.

There is a plane with no gravity and is used for training; It is called the Vomit Comet because it makes people feel sick.

Did You Know?

Jupiter, Neptune, and Uranus all have rings, but we can see only Saturn's because it has ice, and it reflects sunlight.

Pluto takes 248 Earth years to orbit the Sun.

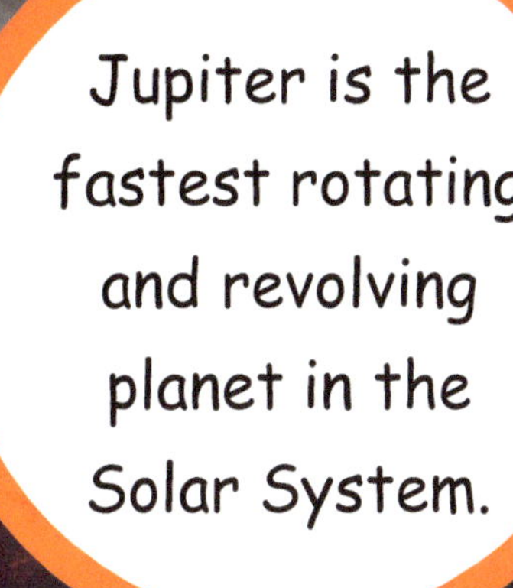

Mars has ice on its surface.

If you melt the ice, the water will cover the whole planet.

Venus is actually called Earths twin because they are almost the same size.

1,000 asteroids hit the Earth every year in the oceans.

The Sun's gravity holds the Solar System together.

The Sun will die in another 5 billion years.

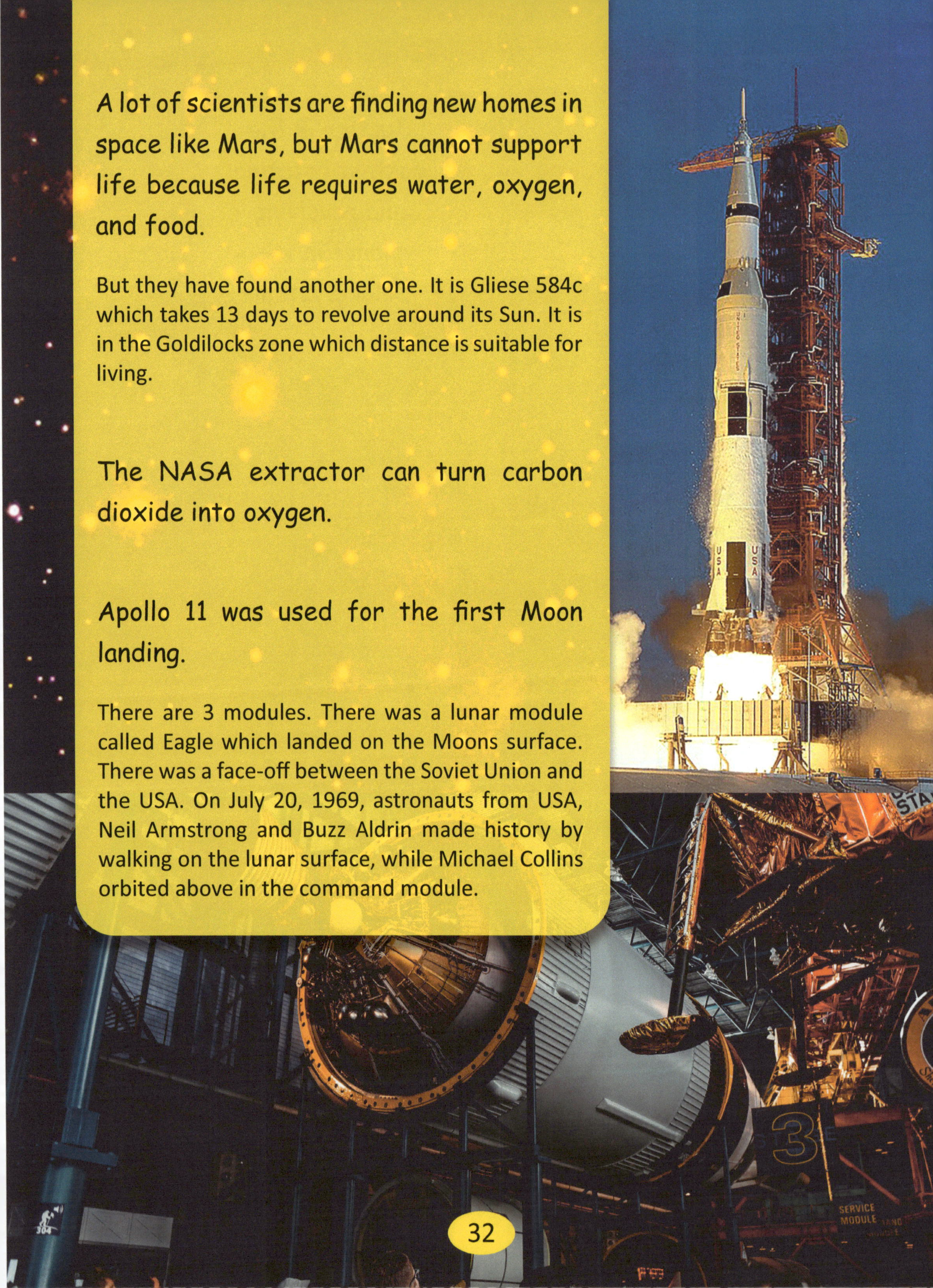

A lot of scientists are finding new homes in space like Mars, but Mars cannot support life because life requires water, oxygen, and food.

But they have found another one. It is Gliese 584c which takes 13 days to revolve around its Sun. It is in the Goldilocks zone which distance is suitable for living.

The NASA extractor can turn carbon dioxide into oxygen.

Apollo 11 was used for the first Moon landing.

There are 3 modules. There was a lunar module called Eagle which landed on the Moons surface. There was a face-off between the Soviet Union and the USA. On July 20, 1969, astronauts from USA, Neil Armstrong and Buzz Aldrin made history by walking on the lunar surface, while Michael Collins orbited above in the command module.

Did you know about the Missions to space?

There have been a lot of missions to space.
Some are

- Apollo 11
- Luna 9
- Sputnik 1 and 2
- Chandrayaan 1, 2 and 3.
  The 4th one is planned.
- Voyagers
- Vostok
- Columbia
- Challenger
- Discovery
- Atlantis
- Endeavour
- Vikings
- Chang'e
- Mars Exploration rovers

And many more
There are even space
stations. Some are

- MIR
- ISS
- There have been 12 people on the Moon.
- There has been only 1 mission to Saturn.

ISRO

ISRO is the short form for **Indian Space Research Organisation**. They have sent many missions to the Moon and 1 mission to Mars.

NASA

NASA's full form is **National Aeronautics and Space Administration** and is from USA. They made the 1st landing on the Moon and have launched many missions to space.

FUN ACTIVITY (COLOUR THE PICTURE)

About the Author

Ayaansh Davda is an 8-year-old explorer at heart and a 3rd-grade student at Mansukhbhai Kothari National School in Pune. He has a big fascination with space and everything beyond our planet. Whether he's stargazing at night or learning about planets and galaxies, Ayaansh's imagination takes him on exciting journeys through the universe.

When he's not dreaming about space, Ayaansh loves to challenge himself with chess and enjoys playing badminton. He's also the proud little troublemaker in his family, always finding fun ways to keep his sisters and brothers on their toes!

Ayaansh hopes you enjoy this adventure through space as much as he enjoyed writing it!

Picture Resources

The author would like to thank the following websites
for the pictures in the book.

https://www.freepik.com/

https://www.canva.com/features/free-stock-photos/

https://science.nasa.gov/mission/webb/multimedia/images

https://webbtelescope.org/news/first-images/gallery

www.ingramcontent.com/pod-product-compliance
Lightning Source LLC
Chambersburg PA
CBHW041607110726
48005CB00002B/317

9798896104674